I0463752

Contents

Welcome to the U.S. Courthouse. During your visit, you'll see judges and their staffs, jurors, lawyers, and people who are involved in court cases. This pamphlet answers some of the questions visitors to the federal courts ask most often. It will help you understand what you see and hear in the courthouse. Of course, legal proceedings are often complex, and a pamphlet such as this may not answer all of your questions.

In the back is a glossary of legal terms that you'll find in this pamphlet. You'll probably hear many of these terms if you attend a proceeding in the courthouse. If you're confused by any of the words printed in boldface in this pamphlet, look in the glossary for a simple explanation.

What Is a Court?

A **court** is an institution that the government sets up to settle disputes through a legal process. People bring their disputes to court to resolve their disagreements: Did Bill Jones run a red light before his car ran into John Smith's, or was the light green, as he says it was? Did Frank Williams rob the bank, or was it someone else?

Courts decide what really happened and what should be done about it. They decide whether a person committed a crime and what the punishment should be. They also provide a peaceful way to decide private disputes that people can't resolve themselves. Sometimes, a court decision affects other people in addition to those involved in the **lawsuit**. In 1965, three high school students in Des Moines, Iowa, were suspended from school for wearing black arm bands to protest the war in Vietnam. They asked a court to declare the rule against arm bands invalid. The Supreme Court decided in the case, *Tinker v. Des Moines School District*, that the rule violated the students' constitutional right of freedom of expression. That decision affected the right of public school students all over the country to express their views in a nondisruptive manner. The Supreme Court's 1954 decision in *Brown v. Board of Education* had an even more widespread effect. The case involved a dispute between the parents of Linda Brown and their local board of education in Topeka, Kansas. The Court decided that requiring white children and black children to go to separate schools violated the Fourteenth Amendment of the Constitution.

1

What Is a Federal Court?

You probably realize that there are both federal courts and state courts. The two kinds of courts are a result of a principle of our Constitution called federalism. Federalism gives some functions to the United States government and leaves the other functions to the states. The functions of the U.S.—or federal—government involve the nation as a whole and include regulating commerce between the states and with foreign countries, providing for the national defense, and administering federal lands and other property. State governments perform most of the functions you probably associate with "government," such as running the schools, managing the police departments, and paving the streets.

Federal courts are established by the U.S. government to decide disputes concerning the federal Constitution and laws passed by Congress, called **statutes**. State courts are established by a state, or by a county or city within the state. Although state courts must enforce the federal Constitution and laws, most of the cases they decide involve the constitution and laws of the particular state.

What Kinds of Federal Courts Are There?

Of all the federal courts, the U.S. district courts are the most numerous. Congress has divided the country into ninety-four federal judicial districts, and in each district there is a U.S. district court. The U.S. district courts are the federal trial courts—the places where federal cases are tried, witnesses testify, and juries serve. Within each district is a U.S. bankruptcy court, a part of the district court that administers the bankruptcy laws.

Congress has placed each of the ninety-four districts in one of twelve regional circuits, and each circuit has a court of appeals. If you lose a trial in a district court, you can ask the court of appeals to review the case to see if the judge applied the law correctly. Sometimes courts of appeals are also asked to review decisions of federal administrative agencies, such as the National Labor Relations Board.

The map of the United States (on the facing page) shows the geographical boundaries of the ninety-four districts and the twelve regional circuits (eleven numbered circuits and the District

Geographical Boundaries of U.S. Courts of Appeals and U.S. District Courts

as set forth by 28 U.S.C. §§ 41, 81–131

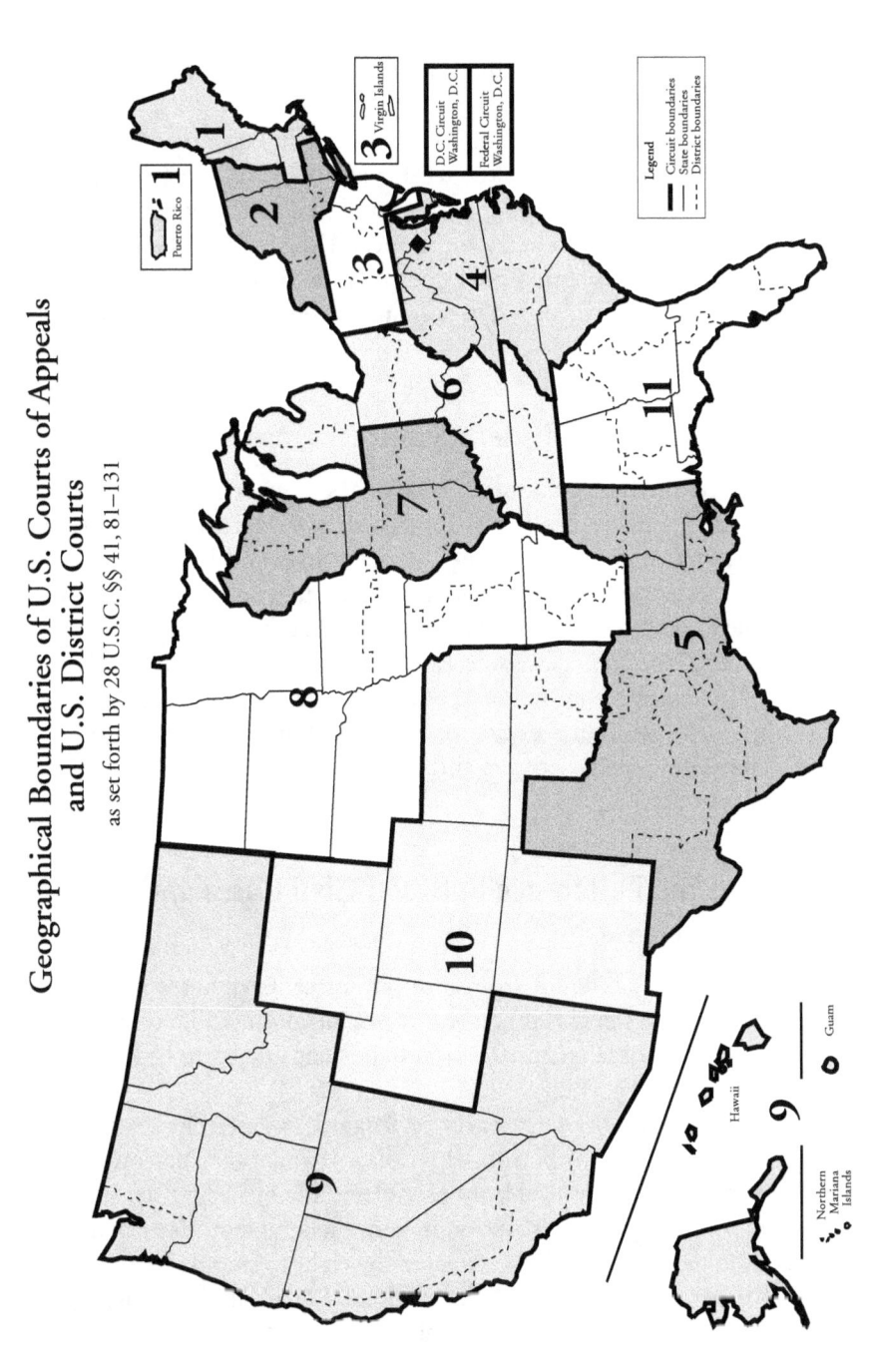

of Columbia Circuit). There is also a Federal Circuit, whose court of appeals is based in Washington, D.C., but which hears certain types of cases from all over the country.

The Supreme Court of the United States, in Washington, D.C., is the most famous federal court. If you lose a case in the court of appeals (or, sometimes, in a state supreme court), you can ask the Supreme Court to hear your appeal. However, unlike a court of appeals, the Supreme Court doesn't have to hear it. In fact, the Supreme Court hears only a very small percentage of the cases it is asked to review.

Who Sets Up the Federal Court System?

Article III of the Constitution establishes a Supreme Court and authorizes whatever other federal courts Congress thinks are necessary. Congress creates the district courts and the courts of appeals, sets the number of judges in each federal court (including the Supreme Court), and determines what kinds of cases they will hear. (Congress has also created courts under Article I of the Constitution, such as military courts and the U.S. Tax Court. But judges of those courts decide only certain kinds of cases and do not have the judicial powers and protections of judges on courts created under Article III.)

What's the Difference Between Civil Cases and Criminal Cases?

Civil cases are different from criminal cases. Civil cases usually involve disputes between persons or organizations while criminal cases involve some criminal action that is considered to be harmful to society as a whole.

Lawyers use the term **party** or **litigant** to describe a participant in a civil case. A person who claims that another person has failed to carry out a legal duty or violated his or her rights, such as those under the Constitution or other federal law, may ask the court to tell the person who violated the right to stop doing it and make compensation for any harm done. For example, Congress has passed a law saying that people have a right not to be denied employment because of their gender. Suppose an employer refuses to hire women as construction workers. Women who had applied and been qualified for jobs might bring a civil case against the employer—sue the employer—for lost wages and seek an order requiring the company to hire them.

Another legal duty is the duty to honor **contracts**. If a lumberyard promises to sell a specific amount of wood to a construction company for an agreed-upon price and then fails to deliver the wood, forcing the construction company to buy it elsewhere at a higher price, the construction company might sue the lumberyard for **damages**.

When a jury (or a judge in cases in which the defendant waived a jury) determines that an individual committed a crime, that person may be fined, sent to prison, or placed under the supervision of a court employee called a U.S. probation officer, or some combination of these three things. The person accused is charged in an **indictment** or **information**, which is a formal accusation that the person has committed a crime. The **government**, on behalf of the people, **prosecutes** the case. It is not the victim's responsibility to bring a criminal case. In fact, there may not always be a specific victim. For example, the federal government prosecutes people accused of violating federal laws against spying because of the danger spying presents to the country as a whole. State governments arrest and prosecute people accused of violating laws against drunk driving because society regards drunk driving as a serious offense that can result in harm to innocent bystanders.

What Kinds of Cases Are Tried in State Courts?

State courts are essential to the administration of justice in the United States because they handle by far the largest number of cases and have the most contact with the public. State courts handle the cases that people are most likely to be involved in, such as robberies, traffic violations, broken contracts, and family disputes.

The state courts have such a heavy caseload because their general, unlimited **jurisdiction** allows them to decide almost every type of case. Jurisdiction refers to the kinds of cases a court is authorized to hear. In recent years, the annual number of state court cases has been roughly 50 million. By contrast, in the same period, about 2 million cases have been brought each year in the federal courts; approximately 80% of these were bankruptcy filings, 15% were civil cases, and the rest were criminal cases. The number of judges in each system further illustrates the difference: There are some 1,700 judges in the federal courts, but more than 30,000 in the state courts.

What Kinds of Cases Are Tried in Federal Courts?

As the preceding numbers suggest, federal courts do not have the same broad jurisdiction that state courts have. Federal court jurisdiction is limited to the specific types of cases listed in the Constitution and specifically provided for by Congress. For the most part, federal courts only hear cases in which the United States is a party, cases involving violations of the Constitution or federal laws, cases between citizens of different states, and some special kinds of cases, such as bankruptcy cases, patent cases, and cases involving maritime law.

Some cases are such that only federal courts have jurisdiction over them. In other cases, the parties can choose whether to go to state court or to federal court. In most cases, however, they can only go to state court.

Although the federal courts hear significantly fewer cases than the state courts, the cases they do hear tend more often to be of national importance, because of the federal laws they enforce and the federal rights they protect.

Most cases in federal courts are civil rather than criminal. As described earlier, one type of federal civil case might involve a claim by a private citizen that a company failed to carry out its duty under the law—for example, that the company refused to hire the person simply because she was a woman. Another kind of federal civil case might be a lawsuit by a private citizen claiming that he is entitled to receive money under a government program, such as benefits from Social Security. A third type of federal civil lawsuit might require the court to decide whether a corporation is violating federal laws by having a monopoly over a certain kind of business.

Appeals for review of actions by federal administrative agencies are also federal civil cases. Suppose, for example, that the Environmental Protection Agency issued a permit to a paper mill to discharge water used in its milling process into the Scenic River, over the objection of area residents. The residents could ask a federal court to review the agency's decision.

There are many more federal civil cases than criminal cases because most crimes concern problems that the Constitution leaves to the states. We all know, for example, that robbery is a crime. But what law says it is a crime? By and large, state laws, not federal laws, make robbery a crime. There are only a few federal laws about robbery, such as the law that makes it a federal crime to rob a bank whose deposits are insured by a federal agency. Examples of other federal crimes are sale or possession of illegal drugs and use of the U.S. mails to swindle consumers.

Federal courts also hear **bankruptcy** matters. Bankruptcy laws enable people or businesses who can no longer pay their creditors as their debts come due to organize their affairs, liquidate their debts or create a plan to pay them off, and get a fresh start. There is a whole code of laws that sets out how the parties involved in a bankruptcy case should proceed: the bankruptcy code. **Bankruptcy judges** decide matters that arise under the code.

How Does a Case Come into a Federal Court?

Courts can't reach out to decide controversies on their own initiative. They must wait for someone to bring the controversy to them. Moreover, courts only decide legal controversies. They are not intended to decide every disagreement that individuals have with one another, or to give advice.

Civil cases. A federal civil case begins when someone—or more likely, someone's lawyer—files a paper or electronic document with the clerk of the court that states a claim against another person believed to have committed a wrongful act. In legal terminology, the **plaintiff** files a **complaint** against the **defendant**. The defendant may then file an **answer** to the complaint. These written statements of the parties' positions are called **pleadings**.

Criminal cases. Beginning a federal criminal case is more complicated. A criminal case usually begins when a lawyer for the executive branch of the U.S. government—the **U.S. attorney** or an assistant U.S. attorney—tells a federal **grand jury** about the evidence that, according to the government, indicates a person committed a crime. That person may or may not already have been arrested when the grand jury meets. The U.S. attorney will try to convince the grand jury that there is enough evidence to show that the person probably committed the crime and should be formally accused of it. If the grand jury agrees, it issues a formal accusation, called an indictment.

A grand jury is different from a **trial jury**, also called a **petit jury**. A grand jury determines whether the person should be released or held for further proceedings; a petit jury listens to the evidence presented at the trial and determines whether the defendant is guilty of the charge. "Petit" is the French word for "small"; petit juries usually consist of twelve jurors in criminal cases and from six to twelve jurors in civil cases. "Grand" is the French word for "large"; grand juries have from sixteen to twenty-three jurors.

After the grand jury issues the indictment, the accused person (the defendant) is arrested, if not already under arrest. The next step is an **arraignment**, where the defendant is brought before a judge and asked to plead "guilty" or "not guilty" of the crime. If the **plea** is "guilty," a time is set for the defendant to return to court to be sentenced. If the defendant pleads "not guilty," a time is set for the trial.

Grand jury indictments are most often used for **felonies**, which are the more serious crimes, such as bank robberies. Grand jury indictments are not usually necessary to prosecute less serious crimes, called **misdemeanors**, and are not necessary for all felonies. Instead, the U.S. attorney issues an information, which takes the place of an indictment. Typical misdemeanors are disturbing the peace (a state misdemeanor) and speeding on a highway in a national park (a federal misdemeanor).

Is There a Trial for Every Case?

Although there is an absolute right to trial in both civil and criminal cases, trials are often emotionally and financially costly, and a person may not want to exercise the right to trial. So usually the parties agree to **settle** the case without going to trial. Some civil cases are decided by the judge, who may decide based on the facts

The Court Systems of the United States

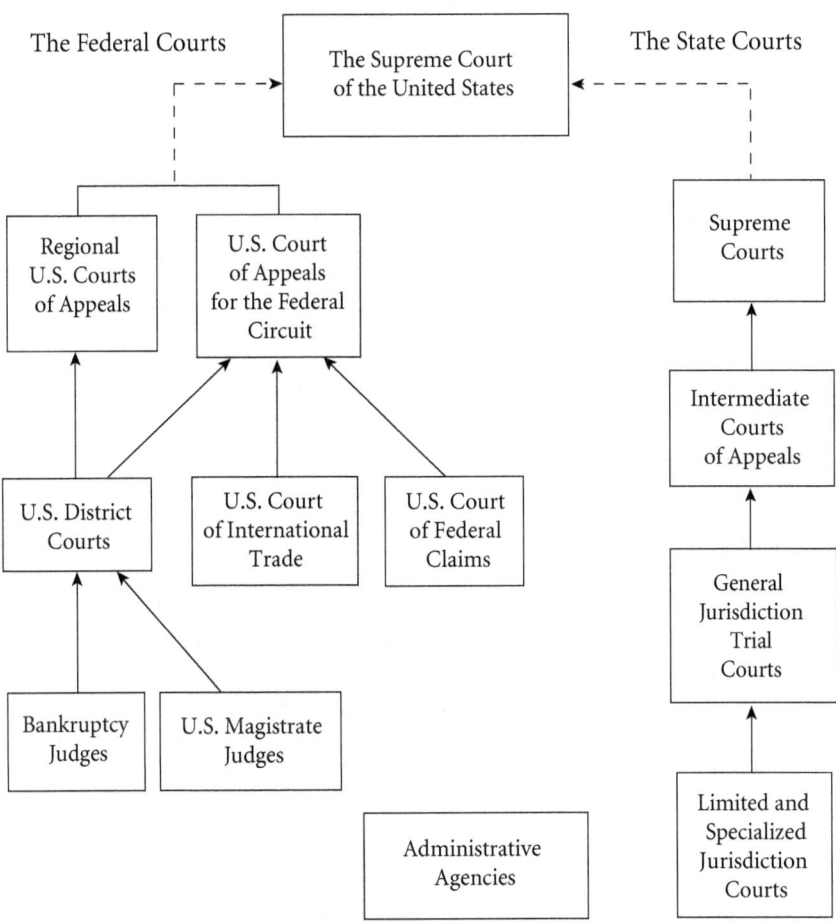

The Federal Courts

The State Courts

The Supreme Court of the United States

Regional U.S. Courts of Appeals

U.S. Court of Appeals for the Federal Circuit

Supreme Courts

Intermediate Courts of Appeals

U.S. District Courts

U.S. Court of International Trade

U.S. Court of Federal Claims

General Jurisdiction Trial Courts

Bankruptcy Judges

U.S. Magistrate Judges

Administrative Agencies

Limited and Specialized Jurisdiction Courts

presented that there is no need to have a trial. Thus, more than nine out of ten civil cases never come to trial, and about eight out of ten defendants in criminal cases plead guilty rather than stand trial. If you watch a trial in progress, remember that what you're seeing is only one part—though a very important part—of the total legal process.

May I Watch a Trial in Progress?

The federal courts are open to the public and have always encouraged citizens to observe trials and other public proceedings. Be sure to remember when you're in the courtroom that the trial is very important to the parties involved, who may lose their freedom or gain or lose a great deal of money as a result of the court's decision. Behave in a manner befitting the formality of the courtroom. Don't talk or laugh during the proceedings, and stand when the judge enters or leaves the courtroom. Exit quietly if the court is still in session when you leave, and comply with the federal court rules that forbid spectators to take photographs or use tape recorders while the court is in session.

What Is the Purpose of the Trial?

Role of judge and jury. If the parties in a civil case can't agree on how to settle the case on their own, or if a defendant in a criminal case pleads not guilty, the court will decide the dispute through a trial. In a civil case, the purpose of a trial is to find out whether the defendant failed to fulfill a legal duty to the plaintiff. In a criminal case, the purpose of a trial is to determine whether the defendant committed the crime charged.

　　If the parties choose to have a jury trial, determining the facts is the task of the petit jury. If they decide not to have a jury and to leave the fact-finding to the judge, the trial is called a **bench trial**. In either kind of trial, the judge makes sure the correct legal standards are followed. If there is a jury, the judge tells the jury what the law governing the case is. For example, in a robbery case in which an unloaded gun was used, the judge would tell the jury that using an unloaded gun to rob a store is legally the same as using a gun that is loaded. But the jury would have to decide whether the defendant on trial was actually the person who committed the robbery and used the gun.

Adversary process. Courts use the **adversary process** to help them reach a decision. Through this process, each side in a dispute presents its most persuasive arguments to the fact finder (judge or jury) and emphasizes the facts that support its case. Each side also draws attention to any flaws in its opponent's arguments. The fact finder then decides the case. American judicial tradition holds that the truth will be reached most effectively through this adversary process.

The **evidence** the jury (or judge, in a bench trial) relies on to decide the case consists of two types: (1) physical evidence, such as documents, photographs, and objects, and (2) the **testimony** of **witnesses** who are questioned by the lawyers.

Standards of proof. The courts, through their decisions, and Congress, through statutes, have established standards by which facts must be proven in criminal and civil cases. In criminal cases (federal or state), the defendant may be convicted only if the jury (or judge, in a bench trial) believes that the government has proved the defendant's guilt "beyond a reasonable doubt." Remember that for the grand jury to issue an indictment, it only has to believe that the defendant probably committed the crime. But for the petit jury to find the defendant guilty, it must be certain that the defendant committed the crime; it can have no "reasonable doubt" about it. A jury verdict must be unanimous, meaning that all jurors must vote either "guilty" or "not guilty." If the jurors cannot agree, the judge declares a **mistrial**, and the prosecutor must then decide whether to ask the court to dismiss the case or have it presented to another jury.

In civil cases, in order to decide for the plaintiff, the jury must determine by a "preponderance of the evidence" that the defendant failed to perform a legal duty and violated the plaintiff's rights. A preponderance of the evidence means that more of the evidence favors the plaintiff's position than favors the defendant's.

Much of the way our court system works can be traced back to developments in England in the seventeenth century, at the time when America was a group of English colonies. During that century, England abolished the hated Court of the Star Chamber, a court that was tied closely to the prosecutor and that brought enemies of the king to trial for treason and other serious crimes, invariably finding them guilty. A century of criminal justice reforms in England resulted in a number of protections for individuals accused of crimes and adoption of the idea that courts should make their judgments free of pressure from prosecutors. American courts inherited these traditions from England and incorporated them into our judicial system.

Who Are the People in the Courtroom?

The judge. The **judge** presides over the trial from a desk, called a bench, on an elevated platform. The judge has five basic tasks. The first is simply to preside over the proceedings and see that order is maintained. The second is to determine whether any of the evidence that the parties want to use is illegal or improper. Third, before the jury begins its deliberations about the facts in the case, the judge gives the jury **instructions** about the law that applies to the case and the standards it must use in deciding the case. Fourth, in bench trials, the judge must also determine the facts and decide the case. The fifth is to sentence convicted criminal defendants.

Federal appellate and district judges are appointed to office by the President of the United States, with the approval of the U.S. Senate. Federal judges come from a variety of professional backgrounds. Some were private attorneys before they were appointed. Some were judges in state courts, federal magistrate or bankruptcy judges, or U.S. attorneys. A few were law professors. Once they become judges, they are strictly prohibited from working as lawyers. They must be careful not to do anything that might cause people to think they would favor one side in a case over another. For this reason, they can't give speeches urging voters to pick one candidate over another for public office, or ask people to contribute money to civic organizations.

Under Article III of the Constitution, federal judges serve "during good behavior." Therefore, they may be removed from their jobs only if Congress determines, through a lengthy process called **impeachment** and conviction, that they are guilty of "treason, bribery, or other high crimes and misdemeanors." Congress has found it necessary to use this process only a few times in the history of our country. From a practical standpoint, almost all federal judges hold office for as long as they wish. Article III also prohibits lowering the salaries of federal judges "during their continuance in office."

The Constitution includes both of these protections—life tenure and unreduced salary—so that federal judges will not fear losing their jobs or having their pay cut if they make an unpopular decision. Sometimes the courts decide that a law that has been passed by Congress and signed by the President, or a law that has been passed by a state, violates the Constitution and should not be enforced. For example, the Supreme Court's decision in *Brown v. Board of Education* in 1954 declared racial segregation in public schools to be unconstitutional. This decision was not popular with large segments of society when it was handed down. Some members of Congress even wanted to replace the judges who made the decision. The Constitution wouldn't let them do so, and today, almost everyone realizes that the decision was right.

The constitutional protection of federal judges that gives them the freedom and independence to make decisions that are politically and socially unpopular is one of the basic elements of our democracy. According to the Declaration of Independence, one reason the American colonies wanted to separate from England was that King George III "made judges dependent on his will alone, for the tenure of their offices, and the amount and payment of their salaries."

Bankruptcy judges and **magistrate judges** are appointed by the courts they serve. They conduct some of the proceedings held in federal courts. They also assist the district judges. Bankruptcy judges handle almost all bankruptcy matters. Magistrate judges often conduct proceedings before trial to help prepare the district judges' cases for trial. They also may preside over misdemeanor trials and may preside over civil trials when both parties agree to have the case heard by a magistrate judge instead of a district judge. Magistrate judges and bankruptcy judges don't have the same protections as judges appointed under Article III of the Constitution.

The jury. The group of people seated in the boxed-in area on one side of the courtroom is the petit jury or trial jury. You won't be able to observe the grand jury during your visit because its proceedings are always secret.

Juries were first used hundreds of years ago in England. The jury was a factor in the events that led to the Revolutionary War. The Declaration of Independence charged that King George III deprived the colonists "in many cases, of the benefits of trial by jury." Thus, our Constitution now guarantees the right to a jury trial to most defendants in criminal cases and to the parties in most civil cases.

In federal criminal cases, there are usually twelve jurors and between one and six alternate jurors. Alternate jurors replace regular jurors who become ill, disqualified, or unable to perform their duties. In federal civil cases there can be from six to twelve jurors. Unlike in criminal cases, there are no alternate jurors. All of the jurors are required to join in the verdict unless the court excuses a juror from service during the trial or deliberations.

The lawyers. The lawyers for each party will either be sitting at the **counsel** tables facing the bench or be speaking to the judge, a witness, or the jury. Each lawyer's task is to bring out the facts that put his or her client's case in the most favorable light, but to do so using approved legal procedures. In criminal cases, one of the lawyers works for the executive branch of the government, which is the branch that prosecutes cases on behalf of society. In federal criminal cases, that lawyer is the U.S. attorney or an assistant U.S. attorney. A U.S. attorney is chosen by the President, with the approval of the Senate, for each of the ninety-four judicial districts. The U.S. attorney also represents the United States in civil cases in which the U.S. government is a party.

Under the Constitution, as the Supreme Court has interpreted it, persons accused of serious crimes who can't afford to hire a lawyer may have lawyers appointed to represent them. In the federal courts, these lawyers are usually from the Federal Defenders Office, a federal agency, or from private defense organizations, or from panels of private lawyers deemed qualified to represent such persons. Although the judge may appoint these lawyers, and they are usually paid with public funds, they don't work for the judge— they work for their client, the defendant.

On relatively rare occasions, defendants in criminal cases or parties in civil cases attempt to present their cases themselves, without using a lawyer. Parties who act on their own behalf are said to act **pro se**, a Latin phrase meaning "on one's own behalf."

The parties. The parties may or may not be present at the counsel tables with their lawyers. Defendants in criminal cases have a constitutional right to be present. Specifically, the Sixth Amendment to the Constitution provides that "the accused shall enjoy the right . . . to be confronted with the witnesses against him." Parties in civil cases may be present if they wish, but are often absent.

The witnesses. Witnesses give testimony about the facts in the case that are in dispute. During their testimony, they sit on the witness stand, facing the courtroom. Because the witnesses are asked to testify by one party or the other, they are often referred to as plaintiff's witnesses, government witnesses, or defense witnesses.

The courtroom deputy or clerk. The **courtroom deputy** or **courtroom clerk**, who is usually seated near the judge, administers the oaths to the witnesses, marks the exhibits, and generally helps the judge keep the trial running smoothly. Sometimes the deputy or clerk is away from the courtroom performing other tasks during parts of the trial. The courtroom deputy is employed by the office of the **clerk of court**. The clerk of court is appointed by all of the judges on the court and works closely with the **chief district judge**, who is responsible for the court's overall administration.

The court reporter. The **court reporter** sits near the witness stand and usually types the official record of the trial (everything that is said or introduced into evidence) on a stenographic machine. (In some courts, the official record is taken on an electronic recorder.) Federal law requires that a word-for-word record be made of every trial. The court reporter also produces a written **transcript** of the proceedings if either party **appeals** the case or requests a transcript to review.

What Happens During a Trial?

Pretrial activity in civil cases. In most cases, the lawyers and judge agree before trial, often at **pretrial conferences**, what issues are in dispute and must be decided by the jury and what issues are not in dispute. Both sides reveal whom they intend to call as witnesses and, generally, what evidence they will introduce at trial. However, just because they agree on these matters before the trial doesn't mean that they agree on how the case should be decided. Rather, the judge holds a conference to avoid wasting time during the trial on issues that can be decided before.

During the pretrial **discovery** process, the lawyers try to learn as much as possible about their opponent's case, as well as build their own case, by asking to inspect documents and talking to people who know something about what happened. If the lawyers have done a thorough job of preparing the case, they shouldn't be surprised by any of the answers the opposing attorney's witnesses give to their questions during trial. One of the basic rules trial lawyers follow is "Don't ask a question if you don't know what the answer will be." The lawyers and witnesses for each side also prepare for the trial by rehearsing their questions and answers.

Frequently, all of this pretrial activity in a civil case results in a decision by both parties to **settle** the case without going through a trial. Settling does not necessarily mean that the parties have reconciled their dispute; they have merely agreed to a compromise out of court. Often it means that the plaintiff has agreed to accept an amount for damages that is less than the amount he or she originally claimed.

Pretrial activity in criminal cases. A good defense lawyer will also conduct a thorough investigation before trial in a criminal case, interviewing witnesses, visiting the scene of the crime, and examining any physical evidence. An important part of this investigation is determining whether the government can use certain items of evidence. For example, the government cannot use evidence that the defendant committed a previous crime to prove that the defendant committed a crime in another case. But there are some circumstances in which evidence of a previous crime may be used. Or, the defendant may argue that the government cannot use the defendant's confession because it was obtained in violation of the defendant's rights. Resolution of these evidentiary issues before the trial can result either in the government's dropping the charges or in the defendant deciding to plead guilty.

Jury selection. If the parties have chosen a jury trial, it begins with the selection of jurors. Citizens are selected for jury service through a process that is set out in laws passed by Congress and in rules adopted by the federal courts. First, citizens are called to court to be available to serve on juries. These citizens are selected at random from lists of all registered or actual voters in the district or from voter lists supplemented by some other sources of names, such as licensed drivers. The judge and the lawyers in each case then choose the persons who will actually serve on the jury.

To choose the jurors, the judge and sometimes the lawyers ask prospective jurors questions to determine if they will be able to decide the case fairly. This process is called **voir dire**. The lawyers may ask the judge to excuse any jurors they think may not be able to be impartial, such as those who know either party in the case or who have had an experience that might make them favor one side over the other. The lawyers may reject a certain number of jurors without giving any justification. Lawyers may not, however, reject jurors on the basis of race or gender.

Opening statements. Once the jury has been selected, the lawyers for both sides give their opening statements. The purpose of the opening statements is to allow each side to present its version of the evidence to be offered.

Direct and cross-examination. Introduction of evidence begins after the opening statements. First, the government's attorney, or the plaintiff's lawyer, questions his or her witnesses. When lawyers question the witnesses whom they have called to testify, it is called **direct examination**. After the direct examination of a government or plaintiff's witness, the defendant's lawyer may question the witness; this is called **cross-examination**. If, after the cross-examination, the plaintiff's lawyer wants to ask additional questions, he or she may do so on a redirect examination, after which the defendant's lawyer has an opportunity for a re–cross-examination. After all of the plaintiff's witnesses have been examined, the defense calls its witnesses, and the same procedures are repeated.

The lawyers often introduce documents, such as bank records, or objects, such as firearms, as additional evidence. These items are called exhibits.

Inadmissible evidence. The courts have established rules that must be observed in court proceedings to determine facts. For example, the Supreme Court has ruled that a defendant's out-of-court confession to a crime may not be used in a trial as evidence of the defendant's guilt if the confession resulted from coercion. The courts adopted this rule because forced confessions obviously aren't trustworthy.

The federal courts have also adopted a rule to prevent repeated injuries to others following a plaintiff's injury. To encourage the defendant to repair the faulty condition that may have caused the injury, the rule forbids the introduction of any evidence of such repair, which could be seen as an admission of guilt. Thus, a lawyer for a plaintiff who slipped on a wet sidewalk cannot introduce evidence that the defendant put up a "slippery when wet" sign after the plaintiff's accident. Without this rule, the act of putting up the sign could be interpreted as an admission that the sign should have been there at the time of the plaintiff's accident and that the defendant had a duty to warn the plaintiff of the hazardous condition. Such an admission would damage the defendant's case.

Another rule concerning the introduction of evidence prohibits the use of secondhand testimony, called **hearsay**. Under this rule, witnesses may not testify to something that they heard about from someone else. If John Smith, for example, testified, "Bill Jones told me he saw Frank Williams rob the Green Valley Bank," the testimony would be inadmissible as evidence. The courts have decided that hearsay is usually not very reliable and, therefore, cannot be used as evidence in a trial.

Sometimes a lawyer will break one of these rules, either inadvertently or on purpose, and will try to present evidence to the jury that it shouldn't be permitted to hear. If an opposing lawyer believes that testimony asked for or already given is improper, the lawyer may object to it and may ask the judge to instruct the witness not to answer the question or to tell the jury to disregard an answer that has already been given. The judge can either sustain the objection and do as the objecting lawyer requests, or overrule it and permit the testimony. When an objection is made, the judge alone decides whether the testimony is admissible.

Occasionally, the judge and the lawyers for both sides confer at the bench—sometimes called at **sidebar**—out of the jury's earshot but with the court reporter present to record what they say. At other times, they might confer in the judge's **chambers**. Often, they are discussing whether a certain piece of evidence is admissible. The court doesn't want the jurors to hear such a discussion because they might hear something that can't be admitted into evidence and that might prejudice them in favor of one side or the other.

Closing arguments and instructions. After the evidence has been presented, the lawyers make their closing arguments to the jury, concluding the presentation of their cases. Like the opening statements, the closing arguments don't present evidence but summarize the most important features of each side's case. Following the closing arguments, the judge gives instructions to the jury, explaining the relevant law, how the law applies to the case being tried, and what questions the jury must decide. The jury then retires to the jury room to discuss the evidence and to reach a **verdict**. In criminal cases, the jury's verdict must be unanimous. In civil cases, the verdict must also be unanimous, unless the parties have agreed before the trial that they will accept a verdict that is not unanimous.

By serving on a jury, citizens have a unique opportunity to participate directly in the operation of our government. Jurors serve as a direct voice of the community in the judicial branch. They also make a vital contribution to the smooth functioning of our judicial system. To encourage citizens to participate, the courts try to make jury service as comfortable and rewarding as possible.

Posttrial matters and sentencing. In federal criminal cases, if the jury (or judge, if there is no jury) decides that the defendant is guilty, the judge sets a date for imposing the sentence. In federal courts, the jury doesn't decide the punishment; the judge does. But the judge's determination is controlled by sentencing statutes passed by Congress and assisted by a set of guidelines, called sentencing guidelines, which take into account the nature of the particular offense and the offender's criminal history. A **presentence report**, prepared by one of the court's probation officers, assists the judge in determining the proper sentence under the applicable rules and guidelines.

In civil cases, if the jury (or judge) decides in favor of the plaintiff, the jury (or judge) usually orders the defendant to pay the plaintiff money (damages) or to take some specific action that will restore the plaintiff's rights. If the defendant wins the case, however, there is nothing more the trial court needs to do.

What Happens After the Trial or Guilty Plea?

A defendant who is found guilty in a federal criminal trial and the losing party in a federal civil case both have a right to appeal their case to the U.S. court of appeals. The grounds for appeal usually allege that the district judge made an error either in procedure (such as by admitting improper evidence) or in interpreting the law.

The government may not appeal if a defendant in a criminal case is found not guilty, because the double jeopardy clause in the Fifth Amendment to the Constitution provides that no person shall "be twice put in jeopardy of life or limb" for the same offense. This reflects our society's belief that, even if a second or third trial might finally find a defendant guilty, it is not proper to allow the government to harass an acquitted defendant through repeated retrials. The government may appeal in civil cases, as any other party may. Also, the losing party may not appeal if there was no trial—if the defendant decided to plead guilty or if the parties settled their civil case out of court. However, a defendant who pleads guilty may have the right to appeal his or her sentence. The government may also sometimes appeal a sentence.

An appeal in a federal criminal case usually proceeds in the following manner: Suppose a law is passed by Congress that prohibits demonstrations within 500 feet of any embassy. Following the enactment of the law, a group of six people stand on a street corner near the embassy of Malandia and ask passersby to sign a petition protesting Malandia's foreign policy. The six people are arrested and charged with committing a federal misdemeanor. At trial, they testify that they were careful to stay more than 500 feet away from the embassy. However, the U.S. attorney calls a police officer as a witness, and he testifies that the corner they were standing on is within 500 feet of the embassy.

Before the trial jury begins its deliberations, the lawyer for the defendants asks the district judge to instruct the jury that collecting signatures on a petition is not a "demonstration" and, therefore, if that was all they did, they weren't violating the law. The defendants' lawyer also argues that the law violates the defendants' First Amendment right to free speech, and therefore the case against them should be dismissed. The judge disagrees on both points.

She instructs the jury that collecting signatures on a petition is a demonstration and refuses to dismiss the case, saying that Congress may prohibit demonstrations that pose a threat to foreign embassies without violating the First Amendment. To reach her decision, the judge consults **precedents**—similar cases that have already been decided by other courts. She pays special attention to prior decisions of the court of appeals for her circuit.

Because the judge has determined that collecting signatures is a demonstration and that Congress has the constitutional power to prohibit a demonstration near an embassy, she instructs the jury to decide, on the basis of the evidence, whether the defendants collected signatures within 500 feet of the embassy.

Suppose that the jury finds that the defendants did collect signatures within 500 feet of the embassy, and the defendants are convicted of violating the law. The defendants may then appeal this decision to the U.S. court of appeals. A court of appeals would rarely throw out the jury's factual finding that the protesters were within 500 feet of the embassy. However, the court of appeals may decide that the district judge wrongly interpreted the law; it may decide that Congress didn't intend for the law to prohibit gathering signatures on a petition. After deciding this, the court of appeals will probably determine that it doesn't have to decide whether it was unconstitutional for Congress to prohibit demonstrations near embassies. That decision will have to wait for a case in which there is an actual demonstration.

If the court of appeals decides that the trial judge incorrectly interpreted the law, as in the example, then it will **reverse** the district court's decision. In other words, the court of appeals will say that the district judge made a mistake in interpreting the law, and thus the defendants are not guilty after all. However, most of the time—but certainly not always—courts of appeals **uphold**, rather than reverse, district court decisions.

Sometimes when a higher court reverses the decision of the district court, it will send the case back to the district court for another trial, or in legal terms, **remand** it. For example, in the famous *Miranda* case, the Supreme Court ruled that Ernesto Miranda's confession could not be used as evidence because he had not been advised of his right to remain silent or of his right to have a lawyer present during questioning. However, the government did have other evidence against him. The case was remanded for a new trial at which the improperly obtained confession was not used as evidence, and Miranda was convicted.

Appellate court procedure. The courts of appeals usually assign a **panel** of three judges to each case. The panel decides the case for the entire court. Sometimes, when the parties request it, or when there is a question of unusual importance, the entire appeals court, sitting **en banc**, will reconsider a panel's decision or hear the case anew.

In making its decision, the panel reviews key parts of the **record** on appeal, which consists of all the documents filed in the case at trial along with the transcript of the proceedings at the trial. The panel then learns about the lawyers' legal arguments from two sources. One is the lawyers' **briefs**. Briefs are written documents (often anything but brief) that explain each side's case and tell why the court should decide in its favor. The second source of information about the lawyers' legal arguments is the **oral argument**. If the court permits oral argument, each side's lawyers have a limited amount of time to explain its case to the judges in a formal courtroom session, and the judges frequently question them about the relevant law.

After the submission of briefs and oral argument, the judges discuss the case privately, consider any relevant precedents, and reach a decision. At least two of the three judges on the panel must agree with the decision. One of those who agree is chosen to write an **opinion**, which announces the decision and explains it. Any judge who disagrees with the majority's opinion may file a dissenting opinion, giving his or her reasons for disagreeing. Many appellate opinions are published in books of opinions called reporters. The opinions are read carefully by other judges and lawyers looking for precedents to guide them in their own cases. The accumulated judicial opinions make up a body of law known as **case law**, which is usually an accurate predictor of how future cases will be decided. Increasingly, the courts of appeals use short, unsigned opinions, which often are not published, for decisions that, in the judges' view, are important only to the parties and contribute nothing to the case law.

If you visit a court of appeals in session, you'll notice how it differs from the federal trial courts. There are no jurors, witnesses, or court reporters. The lawyers for both sides are present, but the parties usually are not.

The Supreme Court of the United States. The Supreme Court is the highest court in the nation. It is a different kind of appeals court—its major function is not correcting errors made by trial judges, but clarifying the law when other courts disagree about the interpretation of the Constitution or federal laws.

Unlike the U.S. courts of appeals, however, the Supreme Court does not have to hear every case that it is asked to review. The Supreme Court decides whether or not it will hear a case. Each year, losing parties ask the Supreme Court to review about 8,000 of the approximately 50 million cases handled by the state and federal courts. These cases come to the Court as petitions for **writ of certiorari**. The Court selects only about 80 of the most significant cases to review.

The decisions the Supreme Court hands down on cases appealed from lower courts set precedents for the interpretation of the Constitution and federal laws that all other courts, both state and federal, must follow. This power of **judicial review** makes the Supreme Court's role in our government vital. Judicial review is the power of any court, when deciding a case, to declare that a law passed by a legislature or an action of an executive official is invalid because it is inconsistent with the Constitution. Although district courts, courts of appeals, and state courts can exercise the power of judicial review, their decisions are always subject to review by the Supreme Court on appeal. When the Supreme Court declares a law unconstitutional, however, its decision can only be overruled by a later decision of the Supreme Court or by an amendment to the Constitution. Seven of the twenty-seven amendments to the Constitution have invalidated decisions of the Supreme Court. However, most Supreme Court cases don't concern the constitutionality of laws but the interpretation of laws passed by Congress.

Although Congress has steadily increased the number of district and appeals court judges over the years, the Supreme Court has remained the same size since 1869, with a Chief Justice and eight associate justices. Like all federal judges, the justices are appointed by the President with the advice and consent of the Senate. However, unlike the courts of appeals, the Supreme Court never sits in panels. All nine justices hear every case, and cases are decided by a majority ruling.

The Supreme Court begins its annual session or **term** on the first Monday of October. The term lasts until the Court has announced its decisions in all of the cases in which it has heard argument—usually until June. During the term, the Court, sitting for two weeks at a time, hears oral argument on Monday through Wednesday and then holds private conferences to discuss the cases, reach decisions, and begin preparing the opinions. Most decisions, with their opinions, are released in the late spring and early summer.

The decisions of the Supreme Court affect the lives of millions of people, from magazine editors trying to decide whether publishing a disparaging article about a famous person may make them liable for damages, to taxpayers whose tax bill may be affected by rulings about state and federal tax laws. The widespread impact of some cases results in lively debates in the media. Rarely does everyone agree with an outcome.

What Are Some of the Most Noteworthy Facts and Concepts You Should Remember About the Federal Courts?

What is most noteworthy varies with an individual's point of view, but everyone should find the following points worth remembering:

- Federal and state courts exist side by side. State courts are courts of general jurisdiction and decide many more cases than federal courts. The federal courts' jurisdiction is much more limited than the state courts' jurisdiction.
- Courts resolve disputes through the adversary process, at both the trial and appellate levels, and rely on precedents for guidance in making decisions.

- Every individual has an absolute right to bring a case in federal court (assuming the court has jurisdiction), along with an absolute right of appeal for review of the district court's decision. Only in rare instances does a case go as far as the Supreme Court of the United States.
- In criminal cases, the courts provide legal assistance free of charge to defendants who cannot afford to pay for it themselves.

Glossary

ADVERSARY PROCESS—the method courts use to resolve disputes. Through the adversary process, each side in a dispute has the right to present its case as persuasively as possible, subject to the rules of evidence, and an independent fact finder, either judge or jury, decides in favor of one side or the other.

ANSWER—the formal written statement by a defendant in a civil case that responds to a complaint and sets forth the grounds for defense.

APPEAL—a request, made after a trial, asking another court (usually the court of appeals) to decide whether the trial was conducted properly. To make such a request is "to appeal" or "to take an appeal."

ARRAIGNMENT (*pronounced* a-RAIN-ment)—a proceeding in which an individual who is accused of committing a crime is brought into court, told of the charges, and asked to plead guilty or not guilty.

BANKRUPTCY—refers to federal statutes and judicial proceedings involving persons or businesses that cannot pay their debts and thus seek the assistance of the court in getting a "fresh start." Under the protection of the bankruptcy court, debtors may "discharge" their debts, perhaps by paying a portion of each debt.

BANKRUPTCY JUDGE—a federal judge, appointed for a fourteen-year term, who has authority to hear matters that arise under the bankruptcy code.

BENCH TRIAL—a trial without a jury, in which the judge decides the facts.

BRIEF—a written statement submitted by the lawyer for each side in an appellate case that explains to the judges why they should decide the case in favor of that lawyer's client.

CASE LAW—the law as laid down in the decisions of the courts; the law in cases that have been decided.

CHAMBERS—the offices of a judge.

CHIEF DISTRICT JUDGE—the judge who has primary responsibility for the administration of the district court, but also decides cases. Chief judges are determined by seniority.

CLERK OF COURT—an officer appointed by the court to work with the chief judge and other judges in overseeing the court's administration, especially to assist in managing the flow of cases through the court.

COMPLAINT—a written statement by the person starting a civil lawsuit that states the wrongs allegedly committed by the defendant.

CONTRACT—an agreement between two or more persons that creates an obligation to do or not to do a particular thing.

COUNSEL—a lawyer or a team of lawyers; the term is often used during a trial to refer to lawyers in a case.

COURT—an agency of government authorized to resolve legal disputes. Judges or lawyers sometimes use "court" to refer to the judge, as in "the court has read the pleadings."

COURT REPORTER—a person who makes a word-for-word record of what is said in a court proceeding and produces a transcript of the proceeding if requested to do so.

COURTROOM DEPUTY or CLERK—a court employee who assists the judge by keeping track of witnesses, evidence, and other trial matters, and sometimes by scheduling cases.

CROSS- (and RE–CROSS-) EXAMINATION—questions lawyers ask witnesses called by their opponents.

DAMAGES—money that a defendant pays a plaintiff in a civil case that the plaintiff has won. Damages compensate the plaintiff for his or her injuries.

DEFENDANT—in a civil suit, the person complained against; in a criminal case, the person accused of the crime.

DIRECT (and RE-DIRECT) EXAMINATION—questions lawyers ask witnesses they have asked to come to court in order to bring out evidence for the fact finder (judge or jury).

DISCOVERY—lawyers' examinations, before trial, of facts and documents that the opponents possess, to help the lawyers prepare for trial.

EN BANC—French for "in the bench" or "full bench." The term refers to a session in which all of the judges on an appellate court (not just a panel) participate in the decision. The U.S. courts of appeals usually sit in panels of three judges, but for important cases may expand the bench to a larger number, and they are then said to be sitting en banc.

EVIDENCE—information in the form of testimony or documents that is presented to persuade the fact finder (judge or jury) to decide the case for one side or the other.

FELONY—a crime that carries a penalty of more than a year in prison.

GOVERNMENT—as it is used in federal criminal cases, "government" refers to the lawyers in the U.S. attorney's office who are prosecuting the case.

GRAND JURY—a group of citizens who listen to evidence of criminal activity presented by the government in order to determine whether there is enough evidence to justify filing an indictment. Federal grand juries have from sixteen to twenty-three persons and serve for about a year, sitting one or two days a week.

HEARSAY—evidence that is presented by a witness who did not see or hear the incident in question but heard about it from someone else. Hearsay evidence is usually not admissible as evidence in a trial.

IMPEACHMENT—(1) the process of charging someone with a crime (used mainly with respect to the constitutional process whereby the House of Representatives may impeach high officers of the government for trial in the Senate); (2) the process of calling the credibility of a witness into question, as in "impeaching the testimony of a witness."

INDICTMENT (*pronounced* in-DITE-ment)—the formal charge issued by a grand jury stating that there is enough evidence that the defendant committed the crime to justify having a trial; used primarily for felonies.

INFORMATION—a formal accusation by a government attorney that the defendant committed a misdemeanor.

INSTRUCTIONS—the judge's explanation to the jury, before it begins deliberations, of the questions it must decide and the law governing the case.

JUDGE—a government official with authority to preside over and decide lawsuits brought to courts.

JUDICIAL REVIEW—this term typically refers to the authority of a court, in a case involving either a law passed by a legislature or an action by an executive branch officer or employee, to determine whether the law or action is inconsistent with a more fundamental law, namely the U.S. Constitution, and to declare the law or action invalid if it is inconsistent. Although judicial review is usually associated with the Supreme Court of the United States, it can be, and is, exercised by all courts. Judicial review sometimes means a form of appeal to the courts for review of an administrative body's findings of fact or of law.

JURISDICTION—(1) the legal authority of a court to hear and decide a certain type of case; (2) the geographic area over which the court has authority to decide cases.

LAWSUIT—an action instituted by a party in a civil court alleging that another party failed to perform a legal duty.

LITIGANTS—*see* PARTIES.

MAGISTRATE JUDGE—in federal court, the U.S. magistrate judge assists the district judges in preparing cases for trial. Magistrate judges may also conduct some criminal trials if the defendant agrees to have the case heard by a magistrate judge instead of a district judge, and they may conduct civil trials when the parties so agree.

MISDEMEANOR—usually an offense less severe than a felony; generally punishable by a fine only or by imprisonment of less than a year.

MISTRIAL—a trial that has been terminated because of some extraordinary event, a fundamental error prejudicial to the defendant, or a jury that is unable to reach a verdict.

OPINION—a judge's written explanation of a decision in a case or some aspect of a case. An opinion of the court explains the decision of the court or of a majority of the judges. A dissenting opinion is an explanation by one or more judges if they believe the decision or opinion of the court is wrong. A concurring opinion agrees with the decision of the court but offers further comment or a different reason for the decision. A per curiam opinion is an opinion for the court not signed by an individual judge.

ORAL ARGUMENT—in appellate cases, an opportunity for the lawyers for each side to appear before the judges to summarize their positions and answer the judges' questions.

PANEL—(1) in appellate cases, a group of three judges assigned to decide the case; (2) in the process of jury selection, the group of potential jurors from which the jury is chosen; (3) in criminal cases, a group of private lawyers whom the court has approved to be appointed to represent defendants unable to hire lawyers.

PARTIES—the plaintiff(s) and defendant(s) to a lawsuit and their lawyers.

PETIT JURY (or TRIAL JURY)—a group of citizens who hear the evidence presented by both sides at trial and determine the facts in dispute. Federal criminal juries consist of twelve persons (sometimes with one or two alternate jurors in case one or more of the twelve cannot continue). Federal civil juries consist of six to twelve persons. "Petit" is French for "small," thus distinguishing the trial jury from the larger grand jury.

PLAINTIFF—the person who files the complaint in a civil lawsuit.

PLEA—in a criminal case, the defendant's declaration of "guilty" or "not guilty" of the charges.

PLEADINGS—in a civil case, the written statements of the parties stating their positions about the case.

PRECEDENT (*pronounced* PRESS-a-dent)—a court decision in an earlier case with facts and legal issues similar to those in a case currently before a court.

PRESENTENCE REPORT—a probation officer's report prepared from an investigation conducted at the request of the court after a defendant is convicted of a crime. It provides the judge with extensive information to determine an appropriate sentence for the defendant.

PRETRIAL CONFERENCE—a meeting of the judge and lawyers in a case to decide which matters are in dispute and should be presented to the jury, to review evidence and witnesses to be presented, to set a timetable for the case, and sometimes to discuss settlement of the case.

PRO SE (*pronounced* pro SAY)—a Latin term meaning "on one's own behalf"; in courts, it refers to persons who present their own cases without lawyers.

PROSECUTE—to charge a person or organization with a crime or a civil violation and seek to gain a criminal conviction or a civil judgment against that person or organization.

RECORD—a written account of all the acts and proceedings in a lawsuit.

REMAND—when an appellate court sends a case back to a lower court for further proceedings.

REVERSE—when an appellate court sets aside the decision of a lower court because of an error. A reversal is often followed by a remand.

SETTLE—in legal terminology, when the parties to a lawsuit agree to resolve their differences among themselves without having a trial.

SIDEBAR—a conference between the judge and lawyers held out of earshot of the jury and spectators.

STATUTE—a law passed by a legislature.

TERM—the time during which a court sits for the transaction of business, also referred to as a session.

TESTIMONY—evidence presented orally by witnesses during trials or before grand juries.

TRANSCRIPT—a written, word-for-word record of what was said, either in a proceeding, such as a trial, or during some other conversation, as in a "transcript" of a telephone conversation.

TRIAL JURY—*see* PETIT JURY.

UPHOLD—when an appellate court reviews but does not reverse a lower court's decision.

U.S. ATTORNEY—a lawyer appointed by the President, in each judicial district, to prosecute cases for the federal government.

VERDICT—a petit jury's decision.

VOIR DIRE (*pronounced* vwahr deer)—the process by which judges and lawyers select a petit jury from a panel of citizens eligible to serve. They do this by questioning the members of the panel. "Voir dire" is a legal phrase meaning "to speak the truth."

WITNESS—a person called upon by either side in a lawsuit to give testimony before the court or jury.

WRIT OF CERTIORARI—an order by a court to a lower court requiring the lower court to produce the records of a particular case tried so that the reviewing court can inspect the proceedings and determine whether there have been any irregularities. The Supreme Court of the United States uses the writ of certiorari as a discretionary device to select the cases it will hear.

The Federal Judicial Center, at the suggestion of the Committee on the Judicial Branch of the Judicial Conference of the United States, prepared this pamphlet for federal courts to have available for use in public education and court visitor programs. The Center updated material in this pamphlet in 2006. It is printed and distributed to the courts by the Administrative Office of the U.S. Courts. Members of the public can obtain copies from their federal court.

The Federal Judicial Center was created by Congress in 1967 as the federal courts' agency for research and continuing education. Its policies are determined by a Board chaired by the Chief Justice of the United States with a membership comprising seven federal judges and the director of the Administrative Office of the U.S. Courts. The judge members are selected by the Judicial Conference.

www.ingramcontent.com/pod-product-compliance
Lightning Source LLC
Chambersburg PA
CBHW051418170526
45165CB00004BA/1869